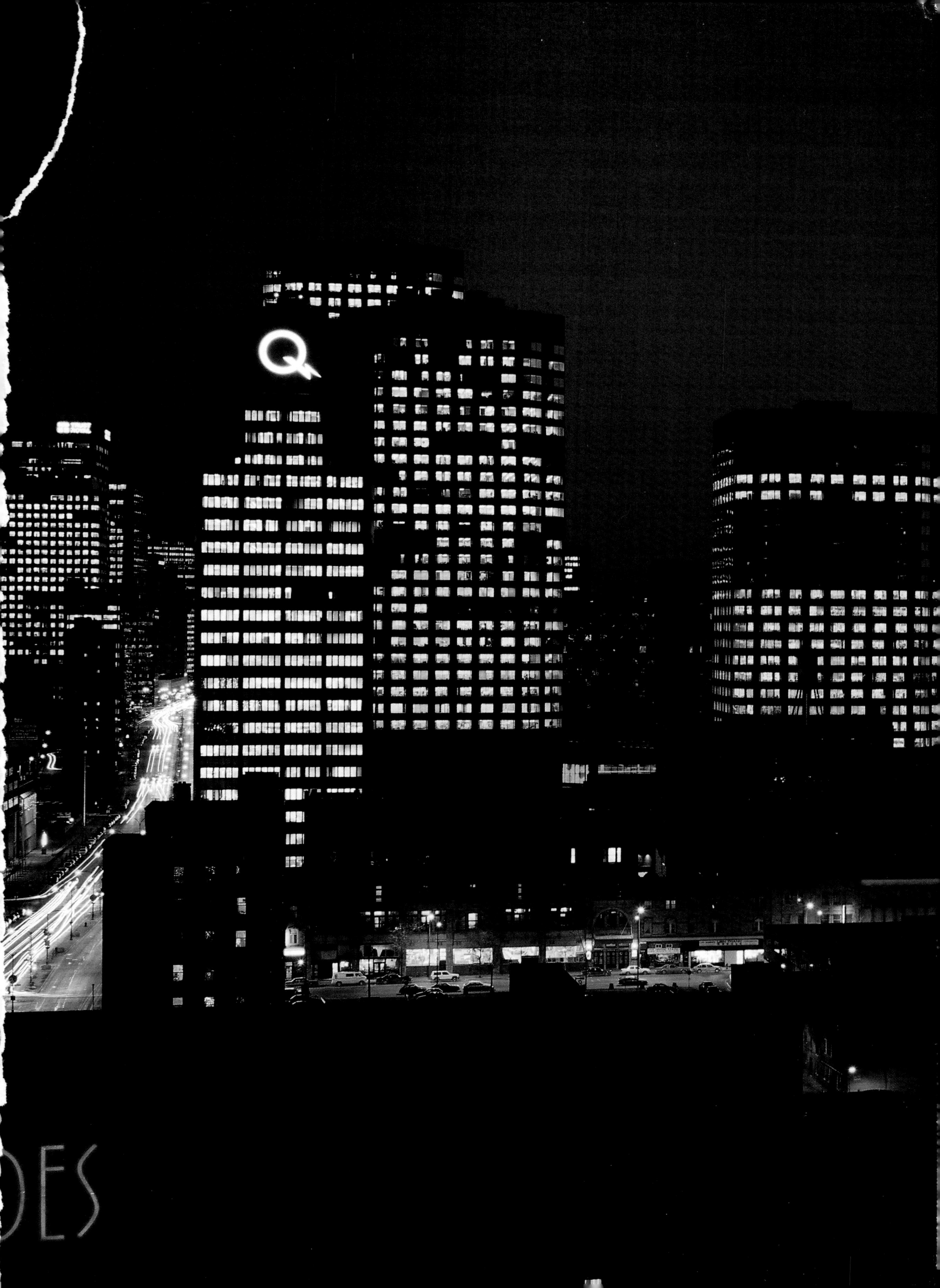
DES

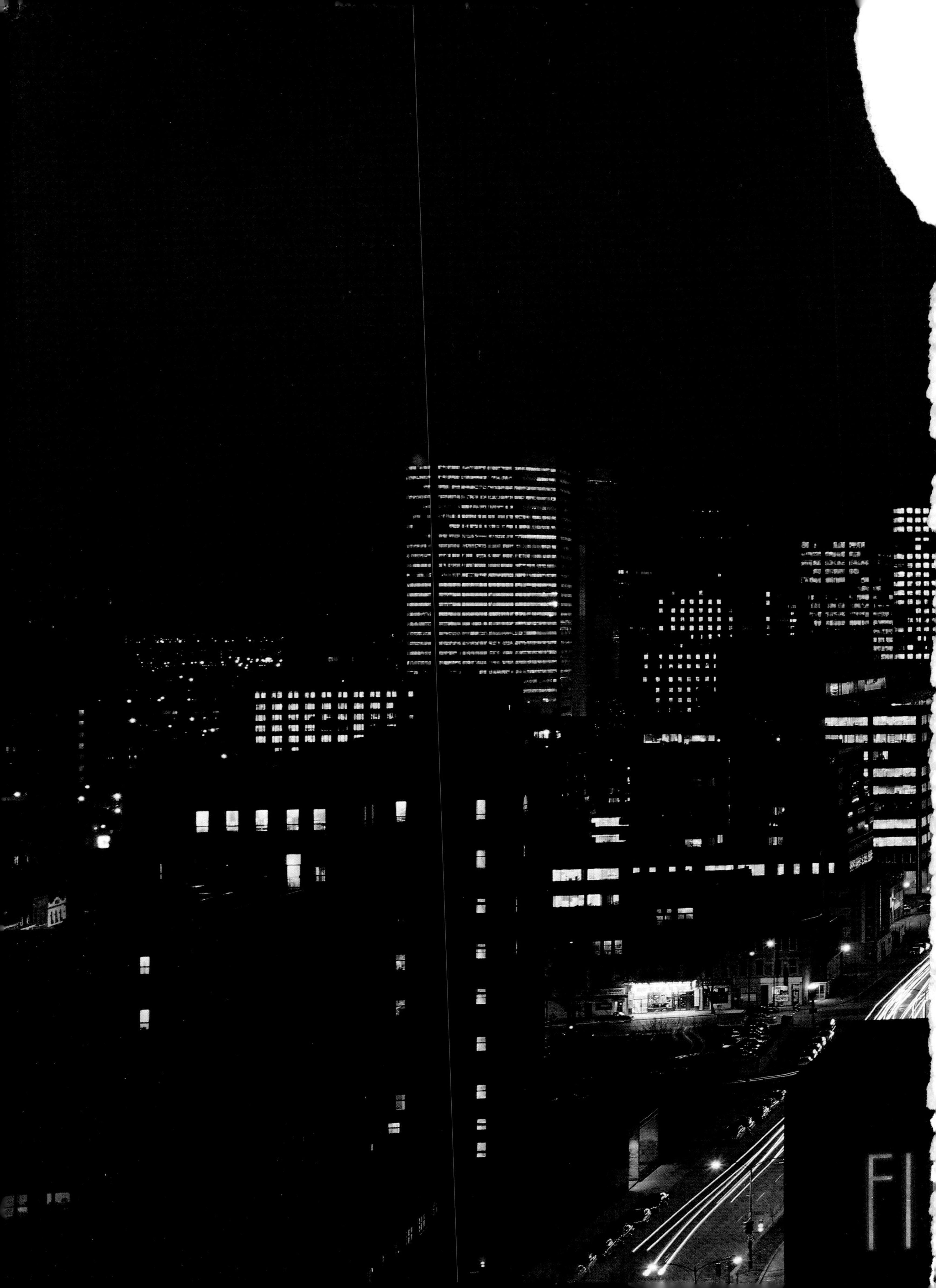

MONT

INTRODUCTION

ARCHITECTURE

THE ARTS

SPORTS AND RECREATION

STREETS AND AREAS

GLIMPSES

THE COUNTRYSIDE

This edition published by
W H Smith Publishers, Canada

Produced by
Bison Books Ltd.
Kimbolton House
117 A Fulham Rd.
London SW3 6RL

ISBN 0-88665-524-2

Printed in Hong Kong

REAL

TEXT	MICHELLE JUSTIN
DESIGN	MIKE ROSE

B. Mitchell

Dedicated to John R Johnson, who never
made it to Montreal, except in his heart.

*3/6 A panoramic view of the city at night, with Mont-
Royal in the background.*

INTRODUCTION

Montreal is a city of subtle richness, quite unlike any other, that seems to defy definition. One half of all Quebecois live in metropolitan Montreal, the cosmopolitan centre of a bastion of French culture in North America. A city of three million people, Montreal dominates the cultural and economic life of Quebec. What is it about Montreal that so captures people, visitors and residents alike? A unique combination of energy and sophistication accounts in part for Montreal's seductive *joie de vivre,* but the key to the city's allure may lie in its history.

The story of Montreal begins in 1535 with Jacques Cartier, who sailed from France in search of a route to Asia and discovered an island in the St Lawrence River. An Iroquois village called Hochelaga lay at the base of a 233-metre mountain which rose majestically from the middle of the island. From the summit of the mountain, which he named "Mont-Royal," Cartier could see miles of fertile plain through which the St Lawrence flowed. To his disappointment, however, the river was barred to the southwest by impassable rapids. These rapids were christened "Lachine," because of the belief that beyond them lay the route to China. Cartier had discovered a natural transportation centre, but it was not until the next century that France recognised its value.

In 1609, Samuel de Champlain, the founder of New France, established a trading post just west of today's Place Royale in Old Montreal. Zealous missionaries followed, attempting to convert the natives to Christianity. The first real colony was established in 1642 by Paul de Chomedey, sieur de Maisonneuve. He brought with him Jeanne Mance, who was destined to establish the first hospital, and a small group of settlers. The devoutly Catholic settlement was placed under the protection of the Virgin Mary and named "Ville-Marie de Montréal."

Life for the early settlers was rugged and uncomfortable. A devastating flood nearly wiped out Ville-Marie during its first winter. Maisonneuve planted a wooden cross atop Mont-Royal in thanksgiving for their survival. Today, a huge steel cross stands as a reminder of Montreal's earliest citizens. One of them, Father Vimont, ended his first Mass with the prophecy, "You are a grain of mustard seed, that shall rise and grow till its branches overshadow the earth."

Settlers persevered through severe winters and incessant fighting with the Iroquois, and many more continued to come, lured by the burgeoning fur trade. Montreal's location, at the junction of the St Lawrence and Ottawa rivers, made it a natural hub for communications and transportation. The St Lawrence River provided the link between the Great Lakes and the Atlantic Ocean. The Richelieu River to the south led to Lake Champlain and the headwaters of the Hudson River.

In 1701, after sixty years of bitter fighting, a treaty was signed and peace was made between the French colonists and the Iroquois. The first half of the eighteenth century was dominated, however, by constant war between the French and English. When Quebec City fell to General Wolfe in 1759, the French moved the capital of New France to Montreal. On 8 September 1760, Montreal surrendered to the British. Its population of 5000 was almost entirely French. The signing of the Treaty of Paris in 1763 marked the official end of the French regime and the start of British rule. The war had ended, but the clash of Anglo- and Francophone cultures was destined to shape the dynamics of the city for the next two hundred years.

Political discontent made peace elusive for Montreal. Americans attempted to take advantage of unrest in the city in 1774. In the hope of expanding their thirteen colonies, members of the First Continental Congress of Philadelphia invited the people of Quebec to send delegates to their forthcoming session. Although the invitation was not accepted, General Montgomery led American troops into Montreal in November 1775. They occupied the city for seven months, fleeing after a defeat in Quebec City when a powerful British fleet sailed up the St Lawrence.

The War of 1812 brought another military invasion by the young republic to the south. American troops, emboldened by victories to the west, opened a new front and again marched on Montreal. The campaign was effectively stopped when Colonel de Salaberry's forces, comprised of British regulars and French Canadian militia, won a victory at Chateauguay, south of Montreal.

Prosperity reigned under British rule. Scottish and British traders reorganised the fur trade and triggered phenomenal growth. The famed *coureurs de bois* and *voyageurs* braved incredible hardships for the merchants, who sent them out to trap and trade in the wilderness. By the nineteenth century,

Montreal was Canada's major commercial metropolis.

In 1841 Montreal became the capital of the United Canadas (Upper Canada, now Ontario, and Lower Canada, Quebec), a title it retained until 1849. The city became the lifeline of an expanding nation. Its port served as the funnel through which the rest of Canada was connected with the Old World. Great ocean ships laden with manufactured goods of every description sailed 800 kilometres up the St Lawrence to deliver their wares to the port of Montreal. Improvements to the port and the development of the railroads fuelled the ever-increasing trade.

The early twentieth century was a period of prosperity and expansion for Montrealers, but the arrival of the Great War brought tensions to the surface. The declaration of hostilities by England immediately plunged Canada into the conflict. French and English alike enlisted in great numbers to support the Crown, but as the war dragged on the call for more troops became more insistent. Conscription was passed in 1917 and was met by protests and riots in the city. The issue was one of many that divided French and English opinion.

Between the wars, Montreal gained a reputation as a second Paris. Prohibition in the United States and much of Canada was defeated in Quebec. Montreal was host to great numbers of American tourists, lured by its fun-loving lifestyle. The liquor trade boomed and so did the renowned nightlife, but the fun was decidely dampened by the advent of the Depression. World War II brought the hardships of shortages and rationing to Montreal, and again the issue of conscription raised protests from French Canadians, who were in turn criticised by English Canada.

The period directly after the war restored prosperity, but local government was widely viewed as corrupt, and areas of the city were downtrodden and poor. The election in 1954 of Mayor Jean Drapeau was the start of a vigorous campaign to place Montreal in the forefront of sophisticated modern cities. A renaissance of the downtown area of Montreal began in the 1960s with the construction of Place Ville-Marie, the first of many underground complexes linked by the city's ultra-modern Metro system. The purpose behind the creation of this "underground city" was to alleviate some of the hardships of the harsh winter months. The city experienced a building boom, and it was during this decade that Place des Arts, Montreal's centre for the performing arts,, was completed. The vision of a thrust toward modernity for Montreal was accompanied by a renewed respect for the past. The restoration of the historic district, Old Montreal, was completed, and today the area charms long-time Montrealers and tourists alike.

Drapeau's most successful scheme to launch Montreal's reputation as a centre of international cultural activity was in 1967. Expo 67, the first officially recognised World's Fair in North America, was a source of pride for all Canadians. The enormously successful Expo was a springboard for the city to host a number of international events. In 1976, Montreal was the site of the Summer Olympic Games. Accompanied by considerable construction, the Games were a great success for sportsmanship, but marred by the tremendous cost that resulted in large, unplanned deficits. The construction of Olympic Stadium was completed in time, but the roof, originally envisioned to be ready for the opening of the Games, was not in place until more than ten years later.

Throughout Montreal's history, the French culture has prevailed, but not without tensions between the city's two main groups. During the thirty-year span of 1941-71, Montreal's population doubled. A migration from the French countryside into the city accounted for much of this growth, bringing unilingual Quebecois to live side by side with Anglophones. The English minority traditionally dominated the business world and held positions of power, while the French majority felt themselves to be victims of discrimination. New immigrants from other cultures gravitated towards English, as it seemed to be the path to success. The Quebecois, surrounded by a sea of English in North America and made to feel second-class in the heart of their own province, feared for the survival of their culture, language, and race.

In 1959, the Liberals, led by Jean Lesage, ushered in "The Quiet Revolution." During this period Pierre Elliot Trudeau and René Lévèsque began to gain prominence in Montreal. The two, of decidedly different viewpoints, would dominate local and national politics throughout the turbulent 1960s and 1970s. Montrealers were swayed by each, and indeed saw no dichotomy in supporting both; Trudeau for the federal government, and Lévèsque for the provincial government. Trudeau was elected Prime Minister of Canada in 1968, and throughout his tenure fought, above all, for a united Canada.

In October 1970 Canadians were shocked when a terrorist group kidnapped James Cross, a British Trade Commissioner, and Pierre Laporte, the Quebec Minister of Labour in Montreal. Cross was eventually freed, but Laporte was murdered, and Trudeau sent riot troops into his home city under the War Measures Act. The actions of the police, marked by violence and brutality, enraged the citizenry.

Rene Lévèsque also eschewed violence but saw the need for a more autonomous Quebec. He founded a political party in 1968, the *Parti Quebecois*, and sent panic throughout Canada when he swept the provincial polls in 1976. He espoused sovereignity-association, which to most Anglophones meant a break-up of Canada. The response in Quebec was cathartic. The articulate Lévèsque gave voice to a people who needed to reassert pride in their heritage and reclaim majority control over their province. French became the official language in Quebec, signs were to be in French only, and English-speaking parents from outside the province were to send their children to French schools.

The political tension resulting from the movement to assert French language rights took its toll on Montreal's economy in the 1970s. Many corporate headquarters moved out of Montreal. During this exodus of Anglophones, investments dwindled, as did the population. By the mid-1980s the trend was reversed, and Montreal's population figures and economy once again took an upward turn. Separation, while always discussed, became less of a burning issue, but enormous change without violence had been accomplished.

Today, Montreal, the second largest French-speaking city in the world, is truly the heart of the province of Quebec. A city of great history by North American standards, its skyscrapers also remind us that it looks ever towards the future. Visitors to Montreal are delighted by the opportunity to experience a taste of Europe in North America. Montreal's fans are fiercely devoted, and their interests range from film to food, from hockey to jazz, from technological research to shopping. Montreal, a vibrant mixture of old and new, is a city of surprises. But more than anything it is a city of warmth, a warmth that permeates even the chill of the Canadian winter.

ARCHITECTURE

Upon arrival in Montreal, the observant visitor is invariably struck by the variety of architectural styles within the city. Montreal has experienced a phenomenal amount of commercial development in the last three decades. Modern structures have changed the skyline along with the character of the city. The outstanding old buildings that have been preserved and protected from the wrecker's ball stand in contrast to recently built ultra-modern skyscrapers. In the presence of a bold, futuristic structure dwarfing a Gothic cathedral, one might expect to feel a sense of conflict or confusion. However, be it a carefully planned result or a fortunate accident, the architecture of Montreal today expresses an overall harmony that is rare in such a combination of styles.

For many, the charm of a city lies in its old buildings. This may be the reason why the historic section of the city, Old Montreal, is so cherished by both long-time residents and first-time visitors. One of Old Montreal's most memorable buildings is Notre-Dame Basilica, a neo-Gothic church designed by New York architect James O'Donnell and opened in 1829. Also in Old Montreal, Notre-Dame de Bonsecours is known as the "sailors' chapel." Grateful sailors left carved wooden ships in the church in thanksgiving for their deliverance from shipwrecks. The chapel balcony overlooks the St Lawrence River and provides an excellent view of Old Montreal and the port.

A short walk from Notre-Dame de Bonsecours is City Hall, an excellent example of Renaissance architecture, completed in 1878 and rebuilt in 1922 after a fire. Across from City Hall is the Château Ramezay. Built in 1705, it was the home of the city's French governors in the early eighteenth century, and later of its English governors. Benjamin Franklin was a resident there between 1775 and 1776, when the American occupying forces, under generals Richard Montgomery and Benedict Arnold, had their headquarters there.

An intricate part of today's Montreal is the "underground city," a network linked by the Metro that extends for nearly 13 kilometres beneath all the major downtown centres. The idea of segregating pedestrians and vehicles began in 1962 with the inauguration of Place Ville-Marie, a 45-floor cruciform tower designed for the Royal Bank of Canada by architect I M Pei, and built over an underground shopping centre. Place Ville-Marie is connected to Place Bonaventure and Place du Canada, and there is access to three major hotels: the Queen Elizabeth, the Bonaventure, and the Château Champlain.

A short Metro ride from the downtown core brings one to the city's magnificent performing arts centre, Place des Arts, and the spacious, airy Complexe Desjardins beneath the Hotel Meridien. One could certainly spend days in Montreal without ever going outside. The complex network provides access to a remarkable collection of restaurants and shops, numerous movie theatres, exhibits, sports facilities, offices and apartments, two train stations, and a bus terminal.

For the student of architecture or the unschooled visitor, there is much to behold in Montreal. It is a city of architectural surprises in its squares, churches, universities, hotels, bridges, train stations, and even its underground. The buildings of Montreal reflect the diversity of the character of the city itself.

15 The Cooperants Building, built in the late 1980's, dwarfs the 1851 Gothic-style Christ Church Cathedral. Beneath them is Place de la Cathédrale, a new shopping centre and part of the underground city.

16/17 Westmount lookout on Mont-Royal provides a magnificent view of the city of Montreal. On a clear day the Adirondack Mountains of New York can be seen beyond the St Lawrence River.

18/19 The domed Cathedral of Mary Queen of the World, also called the Cathedral of Montreal, is a smaller version of St Peter's Basilica in Rome. The tall, cruciform building is Place Ville-Marie.

20 The plaza in front of the Banque Nationale de Paris building is enhanced by modern sculpture.

21 The Seagram Building, on Peel Street in downtown Montreal, dates from 1857. Despite rapid expansion and reconstruction, Montreal has retained some of its finer old buildings.

22/23 Bourgeau designed the exquisitely lavish interior of the neo-Gothic Notre-Dame Basilica. The church houses a huge organ with 5772 pipes, and stained-glass windows depict the religious history of early Montreal.

24 Students of McGill University enjoy a summer day on the lawn. Chartered in 1821, it is the oldest university in Quebec and one of Canada's most prestigious.

25 The Université de Montréal is the second largest French-speaking university in the world. Designed by Art Deco architect Ernest Cormier, it is located on the north side of Mont-Royal.

26/27 Place Jacques Cartier in Old Montreal is dominated by the Nelson Column, an 1809 monument to the English hero. In warm weather, a flower market attracts many people to the cobblestoned square.

28 Houses on Avenue Laval are noted for their mansard roofs, decorated with intricate carvings and colourful tiles.

29 From French Colonial to Art Deco and modern international styles, the Montreal skyline is a study in architectural contrasts.

30/31 Olympic Park, a spectacular sports complex, boasts the world's tallest inclined tower. Facilities include a huge stadium now used for baseball (shown here), a six-pool swimming arena, and a velodrome for cycling.

32/33 The Palais des Congrès adds its futuristic profile to Old Montreal. This advanced convention centre has access to all telematic possibilities, and can accommodate up to 10,000 people.

34 The original buildings of the Royal Victoria Hospital were completed in 1893. Since then the hospital has steadily expanded, and is famed for its high-calibre teaching and research programs.

35 A distinctive landmark on Montreal's skyline, the dome of St Joseph's Oratory is illuminated at night. Many pilgrims left their crutches as a testimony to its reputation as a place of healing.

36 The five-level retail galleria of Place Montreal Trust in downtown Montreal features a large atrium that links the lower levels to the series of terraced levels above.

37 Place Alexis Nihon was built in the 1960s and renovated in the 1980s. The complex now includes a redesigned three-floor shopping centre, office and residential towers, and covered parking levels.

38 The Lionel Groulx Metro station, with its skylights and sculpture. Each Metro station was conceived by a different architect, and many were decorated by artists.

39 Pont Champlain, one of three main bridges into Montreal, reflects the gold of the setting sun on the St Lawrence River.

40/41 A breathtaking view of the city at night, as the rich colours of sunset still linger in the sky.

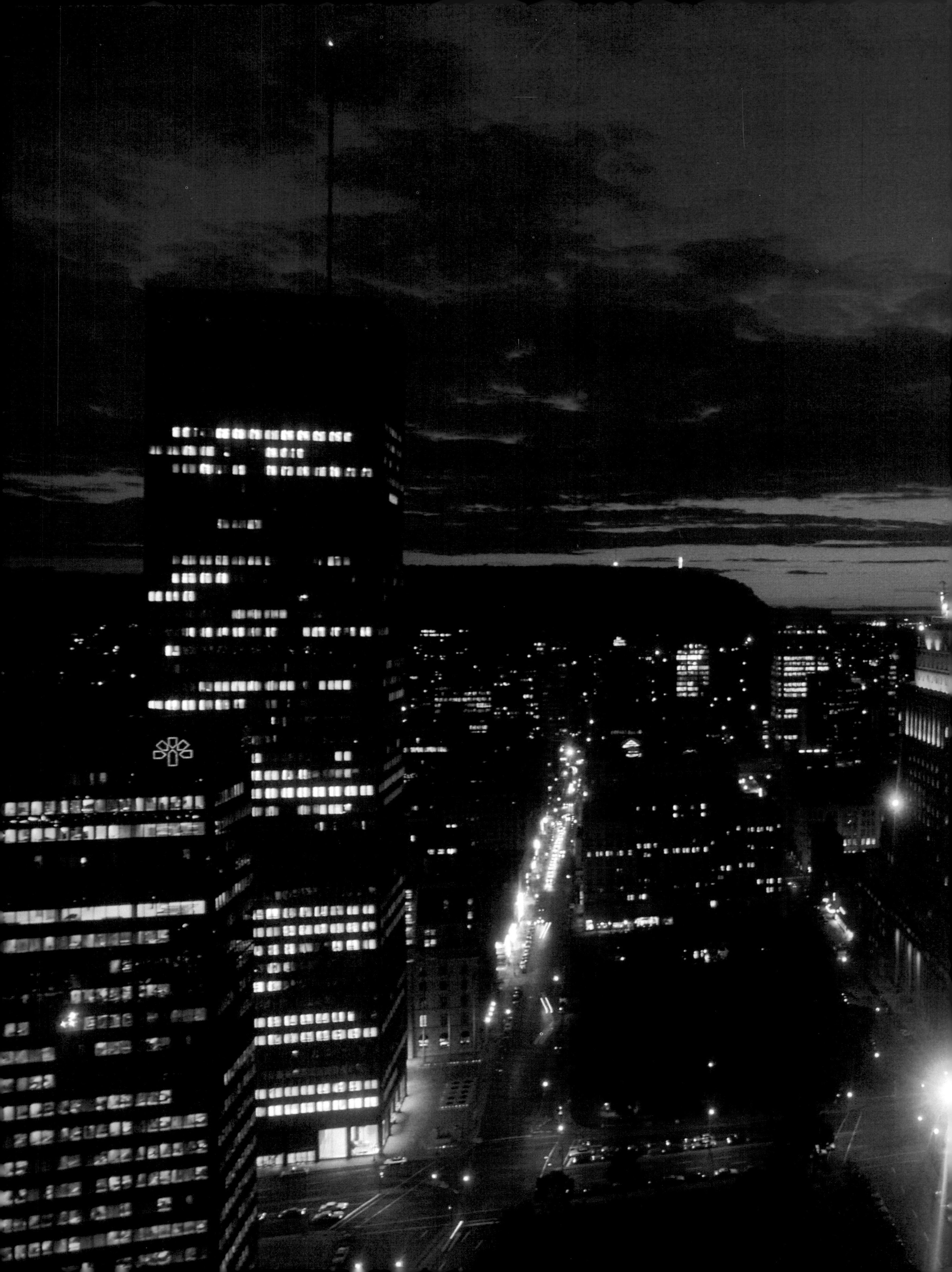

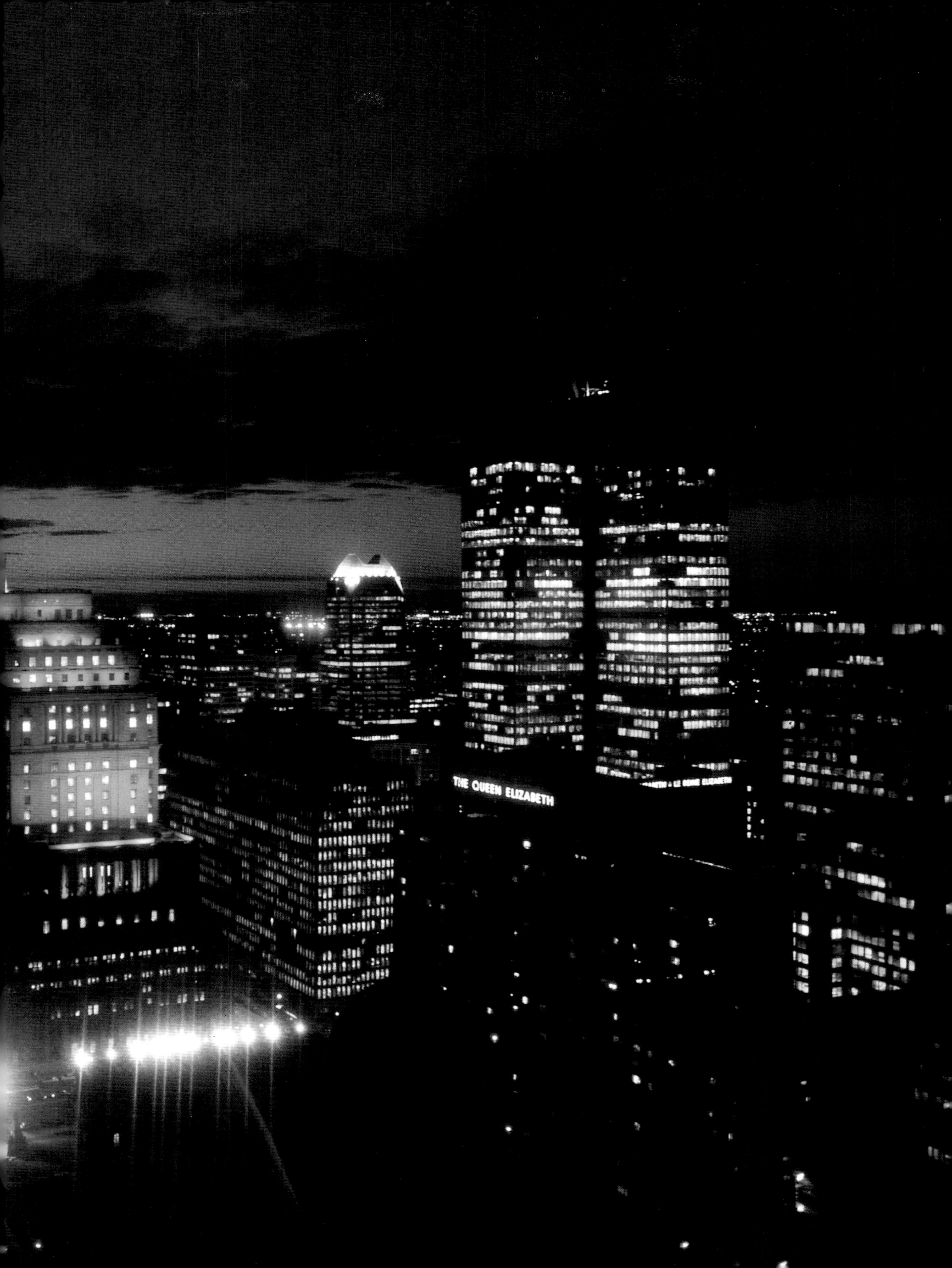
THE QUEEN ELIZABETH

THE ARTS

Montreal serves as a crossroads for French and English cultures in North America, breeding creativity in every area of the arts. The city's magnificent centre for the performing arts, Place des Arts, was inaugurated in 1963. It contains three halls, or theatres, with seating for more than 5000 people. The largest hall, Salle Wilfrid Pelletier, is the site of performances by Les Grands Ballets Canadiens, L'Orchestre Symphonique de Montréal, and L'Opera de Montréal, as well as many world-famous artists.

Montreal attracts many musicians, both popular and classical. It is the home of a world-renowned symphony orchestra whose recordings and tours have won much acclaim. The city boasts three major music schools: the Conservatoire de Musique du Québec, and the music faculties of the Université de Montréal and McGill University. Summer festivals draw musicians from around the world. Over 500,000 people attend the Montreal International Jazz Festival, and the music spills into the streets as the city comes alive with street musicians, acrobats and jugglers. One need not, however, always seek out a concert hall, theatre, or festival in order to hear good music. A visit to a *boîte à chansons* reveals that the people of Quebec have produced some wonderful folk music, with a unique sound and a unique story to tell.

Dance holds a prominent place in the performing arts scene in Montreal. The city's best-known company is Les Grands Ballets Canadiens. The varied repertoire of the company emphasises twentieth-century dance, particularly new Canadian works, with a style that fluidly combines classical ballet and modern dance. Jazz and modern dance are well-represented in the city. Les Ballets Jazz performs at Place des Arts, and some troupes are known for their experimentation and innovations, such as Eddy Toussaint.

Headquarters for the National Film Board of Canada, Montreal is a leading centre for film festivals. The Montreal World Film Festival is a ten-day international competition held in late August and attended by both fans and filmmakers. Montreal is the site of many other film festivals throughout the year, as well as a frequent choice of film location by producers.

Particularly during the brief but pleasant summer, festivals have become a popular form of celebration of the arts. Besides the noted film and jazz festivals, Montreal hosts many other international events, including a Music Festival for Classical Music Lovers, a Mime Festival, and a Puppet Festival. The International Benson & Hedges Fireworks Competition is held for several weeks at La Ronde on Île-Sainte-Hélène. Over the weeks, millions of people pay admission or gather along the banks of the St Lawrence River to view the spectacular pyrotechnical sky shows. The Festival Juste Pour Rire (Just For Laughs Festival) challenges over sixty French and English-speaking comedians from around the world to draw giggles and guffaws from their willing audiences.

The visual arts are very much available and accessible to the public in Montreal. One need merely enter a Metro station in order to see a fine mural, sculpture, or stained-glass window. Museums and galleries abound for every taste. The Montreal Museum of Fine Arts is Canada's oldest, and perhaps Quebec's most distinguished, art museum. Founded in 1860, its permanent collection includes works from pre-Columbian to modern times. Canadian and Quebec art are well-represented, as is Inuit and Amerindian art. Contemporary art can be viewed at the Musée d'Art Contemporain, whose permanent collection dates from 1940 to the present.

43 Les Grands Ballets Canadiens, founded in 1958 by Ludmilla Chiriaeff, is internationally renowned as a trendsetter in twentieth-century dance.

44 The Musée d'Art Contemporain houses a permanent collection from 1940 to the present, and offers exhibitions by contemporary Canadian and international artists.

45 Le Château Dufresne, a classic mansion built in 1918, has housed the Montreal Museum of Decorative Arts since 1979.

46/47 The sky explodes in colour for several weeks in the summer during the spectacular International Benson & Hedges Fireworks Competition.

48 Filmmakers and fans gather at the Cinema Parisien to view the latest trends in cinematography during the Montreal World Film Festival.

49 top L'Orchestre Symphonique de Montréal gives a spirited performance during the International Jazz Festival.

49 bottom French and English comedians coax laughter from the audience during the Festival Juste Pour Rire.

50/51 Place des Arts, Montreal's acoustically superb performing arts centre, is the home of L'Orchestre Symphonique de Montréal, L'Opéra de Montréal, and Les Grands Ballets Canadiens.

52 The International Jazz Festival attracts big-
name artists from fifteen countries, as well as
many brilliant lesser-knowns and street musicians.

53 A local artist sets up a sidewalk exhibit in Old
Montreal, where sketches of the charming buildings are popular souvenirs for tourists.

SPORTS AND RECREATION

When speaking of sports in Montreal, it would be an injustice not to begin with a discussion of what is undeniably the city's dominant sport: hockey. From October to April, faithful fans gather at the Montreal Forum to watch the Canadiens battle their National Hockey League rivals. The game of hockey in Canada dates back to at least 1855. It has created its share of heroes, as well as fiercely determined fans, some of whom in 1955 rioted in the streets when Maurice 'Rocket' Richard was suspended from the Stanley Cup playoffs. Since that year, the Montreal Canadiens have dominated the Stanley Cup competition. Hockey is played in Montreal at every neighbourhood rink, with each young player dreaming of his chance to play someday at the Forum.

In the hearts of many of Montreal's sports fans, the arrival of spring signals more than the end of the hockey season. The perennial sound of the crack of the bat is heard each spring at Olympic Stadium, when the Montreal Expos begin their season in the National Baseball League. Mention of Olympic Stadium brings more to mind than just baseball. The stadium is part of a magnificent complex built for the 1976 Summer Olympic Games. Although damaged by tales of scandal, expense, and incompetence during its construction, the complex stands as a spectacular facility for swimming, cycling, roller skating, ice skating, tennis, equestrian events, and, of course, baseball.

Racing is another extremely popular sport in Montreal. Harness racing takes place year-round at the Blue Bonnets racetrack. Each June, the Canadian Grand Prix gives Formula One drivers the opportunity to compete for the world championship on the 4.4 kilometre Gilles Villeneuve Circuit on Île Notre-Dame. Runners look forward to the 42.195-kilometre course through the streets of the city when the Montreal International Marathon takes place in early September. Montreal is also the home of many devoted cyclists and the site of the Grand Prix des Amériques.

Montreal winters may seem lengthy, but not overly so for those who participate in the many available winter sports. Skiing, both cross-country and alpine, rivals ice skating as the city's most popular winter activity. Cross-country skiers take advantage of the ever-present snow throughout the city's parks and golf courses. On a crisp winter day skiers can be seen on the Metro on their way to the trails of Île Sainte-Hélène or Île Notre-Dame. For those who prefer the thrill of downhill skiing, the city offers seven alpine slopes. Another popular method of travelling from the top of a hill to the bottom is the toboggan. Ice skates replace shoes and boots at the numerous neighbourhood park rinks, or on a canal at Île Notre-Dame. At night, skaters can be found on any one of the city's 29 illuminated rinks.

The warm weather not only brings Montrealers to the outdoor cafés, but also to parks and surrounding lakes. Just west of the city is Lachine, where rafters and jet-boaters test the rapids. Boats take to the rivers and lakes of the city and its surrounding areas, propelled by sails, oars, and motors.

Lovers of the outdoors who are in pursuit of tranquillity, or at least less strenuous activities, find their way to Montreal's many beautiful parks. Park Mont-Royal was designed by New York's Central Park landscape architect Frederick Law Olmsted. With two major peaks, it offers a panoramic view of the city and beyond. Park LaFontaine and Park Angrignon are also popular, for the respite they offer from hectic city life.

55 Montreal's National Hockey League team, the Canadiens, is a multiple winner of the Stanley Cup.

56 top With or without a toboggan, Montrealers know how to have fun in the snow.

56 bottom The city's parks provide excellent cross-country ski trails, particularly on Île Notre-Dame, Île Sainte-Hélène, and Mont-Royal.

57 Most children in Montreal learn to skate shortly after they learn to walk. Every neighbour-hood park has a skating or hockey rink.

58 The nearby Laurentians offer exciting downhill skiing to novices and experts alike.

59 Skating is a popular winter activity on Montreal's many outdoor rinks.

60/61 A quiet moment in autumn at Beaver Lake on "The Mountain," Mont-Royal. The man-made lake is a favourite spot for skating in winter and sailing miniature boats in summer.

62 Summer visitors to Park LaFontaine enjoy boating on the lake.

63. Picnickers flock to Montreal's parks in the summer. At Angrignon Park, children take off their shoes to feel the cool water as it tumbles into the lake.

64/65 At the Grand Prix on Île Notre-Dame, top Formula 1 drivers compete for the world championship.

66 *Tim Raines of the Montreal Expos, who play their National League rivals at Olympic Stadium.*

67 *Montreal's newest soccer team, the Supras, help to strengthen the game's increasing popularity.*

68 Ice fishing on the frozen lakes and rivers of
the Montreal area is a popular winter sport.

69 An excursion on the Lachine Rapids, an exciting way to spend a summer afternoon.

*70 The sun lays a jewelled path between sailors
on Lac St-Louis.*

71 Rowers ply the waters of the Olympic rowing
basin on Île Notre-Dame.

STREETS AND AREAS

Montreal is comprised of a series of sections, indeed neighbourhoods, each with its own unique spirit and characteristics. The city sits on an island in the St Lawrence River, roughly 40 kilometres long and 15 kilometres wide. Its most distinctive natural feature is the mountain in the middle of the island, Mont-Royal, which provides a view of Montreal.

In the south central section of the island is the core of Montreal, the downtown area. Sherbrooke Street, the city's most fashionable street, borders the downtown core to the north. Roddick Gates mark the entrance to McGill University, which owns many of the fine old mansions along the street. Numerous elegant boutiques and art galleries have contributed to the street's reputation for exclusivity. Trendy Crescent Street is renowned among Montrealers for its nightlife, along with neighbouring Bishop, Mackay and Mountain. Ste-Catherine Street, Montreal's main commercial thoroughfare, is the site of the city's major department stores, including Eaton's, Simpson's, and The Bay.

Montreal's Latin Quarter is so-called because of the large student population that frequents St-Denis Street and the surrounding area. This is a younger, French counterpart to Crescent Street, with many of the students coming from the Université du Québec à Montréal. St-Denis Street is lined with bistros, cafés, and restaurants.

The Prince Arthur pedestrian mall, known for its many inexpensive restaurants, is particularly lively on summer nights, when people vie for sidewalk or window tables to watch street performers. There is a large Portuguese population in the St-Louis district, and brightly-coloured houses and outdoor staircases are frequent sights.

One out of every five people in Montreal was born outside of Quebec. Nowhere is this more evident than on Boulevard St-Laurent. Called "The Main," it divides the island of Montreal into east and west. Predominantly a Jewish district in the beginning of the twentieth century, the Main is now likened to a miniature Europe. During the day the street is a marketplace filled with the myriad sounds and smells of the languages and foods of Eastern Europe, Greece, Latin America, Portugal, Germany, Spain, and more.

The historic section of the city exudes charm from its cobblestoned squares and old buildings. Old Montreal is the site of the founding of Ville-Marie in 1642 by Paul de Chomedey, sieur de Maisonneuve. Historic landmarks, museums, and churches stand amid elegant French restaurants, rustic bistros, and simple cafés. At the foot of Place Jacques Cartier in Old Montreal is the Old Port, the site of a summer festival of free events. Crowds gather to see plays, movies, puppet shows, and clowns. At night, rock or classical music fills the air over the St Lawrence River.

Across the Jacques Cartier Bridge are Île Sainte-Hélène and Île Notre-Dame. The two islands were the site of Montreal's world exhibition, Expo 67, some of which has been retained as an annual summer fair, Man and His World. La Ronde, an exciting and colourful amusement park complete with bars and restaurants, is maintained on Île Sainte-Hélène. Île Notre-Dame is the site of Montreal's Grand Prix racetrack, the Gilles Villeneuve Circuit. The Olympic rowing basin, the museum Palais de la Civilisation, and a floral park begun in 1980 with the Floralies Internationales exhibition are here as well. Both islands are favourite spots in the winter for ice skaters, cross-country skiers, and snowshoers.

Finally, outside the city to the west is the Lakeshore. Charming West Island towns extend along St-Joseph Boulevard and Lakeshore Drive from Lachine, where jet-boaters and rafters test the river's rapids, to the picturesque Pointe-Claire and Sainte-Anne de Bellevue.

73 The Prince Arthur pedestrian mall comes alive with street entertainment in the summer months. Popular for its many ethnic, bring-your-own-wine restaurants, the area is ideal for people-watching.

74 Les Halles, on Crescent Street, is reputed to be one of Montreal's finest restaurants.

75 The townhouses on this segment of Crescent Street have become elegant boutiques and art galleries. Just a short walk down Crescent brings one to the west-end centre of the city's vibrant nightlife.

76 top St-Denis Street, a popular student area, is the French counterpart to Crescent Street. The street is lined with shops, cafés, bistros, and restaurants.

76 bottom The Faubourg Ste-Catherine is a market-style shopping centre known for its specialty food shops.

77 Boulevard St-Laurent, or The Main, is a bustling centre of ethnic diversity. Each day the street takes on the atmosphere of a European bazaar.

78/79 Ste-Catherine Street changes from a major shopping district during the day to a centre of exuberant nightlife with its many restaurants, discotheques, and bars.

80 Montreal's major public markets are most active on Saturdays. Jean Talon Market, in the Italian district, is known for its butcher shops and
cheese stalls as well as its fresh produce.

81 Flowers and fresh fruits and vegetables are
the specialty of the farmer's market at Maisonneuve.

82 Only about 300 of Montreal's Chinese population of 25,000 live in Chinatown. The area is fre-
quented by seekers of excellent, inexpensive
food.

83 The Caffé Italia, in the city's charming Italian
district.

84/85 Habitat 67 imposes unique architectural lines on the landscape.

86 *A woman walks her dog along one of Westmount's winding roads on a serene winter afternoon.*

87 This ivy-covered stone mansion is one of
Westmount's many handsome dwellings.

88 An aerial view of Île Notre-Dame, the site of Expo 67.

89 La Ronde, an exhilarating amusement park built for Expo 67, is maintained on Île Sainte-Hélène. Among its many exciting rides is "The Monster," one of the world's highest rollercoasters.

90/91 The Old Port offers summer-long entertainment with concerts, dance, and mime shows. The clock tower was built in 1919 as a monument to sailors who perished at sea.

92/93 Montreal's average temperature in January is − 10°C. The Seaway closes during the cold winter months when the St Lawrence River freezes over, and ice skaters take to the canals.

GLIMPSES

Perhaps the best way to explain Montreal is, indeed, through glimpses. There is no manual of step-by-step instructions to the discovery of the essence of its rarity. The quest requires all five senses, and then some. Pause at the top of Mont-Royal and glimpse the city's grandeur. Stand in front of a monument in a square in Old Montreal and glimpse the city's history. Or step in time to the syncopated beat of a summer night as you take a walk on St-Denis Street. Or grab a shopping bag and spend an afternoon on The Main or at Marché Jean Talon. Or sit in a chalet on the outskirts of the city on a December night and watch the snowflakes fall through a spotlight as you sip a glass of cognac. The key lies in abandonment. You must let yourself grab onto the sleeve of Montreal's vivacious nature, relax, and go with it. Along the way you will encounter the pieces of the puzzle and assemble them for yourself.

Montreal is winter. Icicles form sculptures suspended until spring from the rooftops. Bells jingle as a horse-drawn sleigh ascends the mountain. The wind drives the falling snow until the night sky turns white. A cheerful camaraderie always seems to follow a snowstorm, along with the battalions of plows that handle it so efficiently. There is no bluer sky than the one over Montreal on a clear winter day and no colder chill than a gust of the wind over the St Lawrence. In the words of Gilles Vigneault, "Mon Pays, n'est pas un pays, c'est l'Hiver."

Montreal is sensual. It is a city of lovers, where couples hold hands in cafés and kiss on the street. Food is taken very seriously, be it *patates frites* and a bottle of beer or haute cuisine and a bottle of Bordeaux. Musicians perform in concert halls and in Metro stations in the parks and on the streets. Colour is the rule by day with vividly painted buildings, and by night with the city lights.

Montreal is faces. A chic woman glances out of the window of a stylish shop. A rosy-cheeked child laughs with delight as she careens down a snow-covered hill. Immersed in her task, a greenhouse gardener frowns as she coaxes blooms to brighten a gray winter's day. A white-faced mime pauses, momentarily frozen in tragicomic silence. A shopkeeper grins over the top of his rows of fresh fruits. Determined and intense, animated and serene, mischievous and friendly, the variety is endless.

It is said that no one ever visits Montreal once. Poke in and out of its corners and discover its charms by delightful accident. Montreal, in all its sophistication and cosmopolitan grace, is still, to many who live there, a small town.

95 A table at the window of a charming café is the perfect place to pass a summer afternoon in Montreal.

96 Prince Arthur Street has many brightly-painted, well-preserved buildings such as this one.

97 Icicles embellish the intricate details of the façade of this Tupper Street house.

98/99 Murals such as these on Bleury Street (above) and Prince Arthur Street (right) contribute to the city's colour and character.

100

100 top Ben's Deli is a downtown institution, known far and wide for its smoked meat.

100 bottom Hot bagels come out of the ovens 24 hours a day at the Fairmount Bagel Factory.

101 A neighbourhood grocery store artfully displays its fresh fruits in the window.

102/103 The perpetual motion of St-Denis Street at night.

and
Cafe
BRUNCH
8$
DE 11H30 A 3H
GRATUIT POUR
LER ENFANTS
ACCOMPAGNES

104/105 Outdoor cafés, or terrasses, are as much a symbol of Montreal as they are of Paris. Prince Arthur becomes one large terrasse in the summertime.

105 Montreal is one of the great culinary capitals of the world. Diners on the porch of this French restaurant savour the pleasant weather, conversation, and a leisurely lunch.

106 A casually dressed couple chats in front of the massive wooden doors of Notre-Dame Basilica.

107 A horse-drawn carriage, or calèche, passes the stunning, Renaissance-style City Hall. Calèches are a familiar sight in Old Montreal, Dominion Square, and on Mont-Royal.

108 The bare branches of a tree are beautifully etched against the shadowy figure of a church spire. As the snow falls the city takes on the silver-gray colour of the sky.

109 A sculpture in front of a Sherbrooke Street gallery serves as a somewhat comical reminder that, for Montrealers, life goes on as usual during a snowstorm.

110 At Place d'Armes in Old Montreal stands the statue of Maisonneuve, marking the site of a 1644 battle between the French and the Iroquois Indians.

111 The steel cross atop Mont-Royal is a dramatic symbol of the early founders of the city.

112/113 Montrealers, and the city itself, are an enigma—always full of surprises, yet relaxed, warm, proud, and confident.

114

114 Some of the many animated faces of Montreal.

115 The garden restaurant of the Ritz Carlton Hotel attracts a well-heeled clientele.

116 Mont-Royal is a perfect place to spend a
quiet day sitting in the sunshine or riding in a
calèche.

117 The Botanical Gardens feature over 30 outdoor gardens and ten greenhouses, including a
large collection of bonsai. Here a young woman
tends to a bed of bright purple blooms.

THE COUNTRYSIDE

A drive outside of Montreal need not be a particularly long one in order to find beautiful countryside. Within an hour to the north or southeast lie two natural playgrounds: the Laurentians, and the Eastern Townships. In any season, these areas are a delight to Montrealers in search of a respite from city life, and to tourists in search of Quebec's natural beauty. For those seeking active diversions, golfing, sailing, swimming, camping, hiking, boating, and fishing are all warm weather attractions. Cross-country and alpine skiers are never disappointed during the winter months.

The Eastern Townships, or l'Estrie, have been called the "Garden of Quebec." Farmhouses nestle amongst rolling hills and clusters of lakes. The region is reminiscent of New England, settled by Loyalists who came north after the Revolutionary War. In the 1790's, Loyalists founded Sherbrooke, now the main city of the region.

Fall's colours are spectacular here, and many autumn visitors stop in Granby, the gateway to the area, for the Festival Gastronomique. The town also attracts people to its zoo and its car museum, which houses a fine collection of antique autos. When spring comes to the Townships the sap runs, and sugaring-off festivals produce the finest maple syrup.

The lake areas are most popular in the summer. Memphremagog, whose Indian name means "beautiful waters," is the largest lake. The nearby abbey, St Benoit-du-Lac, offers cheeses made by Benedictine monks. Mont Orford Provincial Park has an outstanding arts centre, where exhibitions and classical concerts are held during the summer. Also held here are the Canadian Hang-Gliding Championships. Mont Orford itself, 792-metres high, draws many skiers during the winter. Other excellent slopes in the Eastern Townships can be found at Sutton, Owl's Head, and Glen Mountain.

The Laurentian Mountains, one of the oldest mountain ranges in the world, lie to the north of Montreal. The mountains were formed more than 600 million years ago, and lakes and rivers were carved through the area by glaciers. The Laurentians are renowned for fine restaurants and resorts. With its many lakes and thick forests, the region is a photographer's paradise. In warm weather, activities include tennis, golf, horseback riding, cycling, and all water sports. A magnificent ski area in the winter, the highest peak of the Laurentians and most popular among skiers is the 960-metre Mont Tremblant. Other popular winter sports include snowshoeing, skating, cross-country skiing, sleigh riding, and snowmobiling. North of Mont Tremblant is a provincial park with the same name, comprised of over 1500 square kilometres of lakes and woods, and home to over 30 species of animals. The largest town in the Laurentians is Ste Agathe, where Lac des Sables offers an idyllic picnic spot. Most of the area's resorts lie between Ste Agathe and St Jerome, which was established in 1830. Curé Labelle, a nineteenth-century priest who is now a folk hero, foresaw the region's possibilities and helped to establish many of its communities. The Laurentians, with all of its tourist activity, still remains an area unspoiled by man. Large sections are wildlife reserves, and much care has been taken to preserve the environment.

119 A church in Mont Tremblant is nearly buried in a midwinter snowdrift.

120/121 One of Park Mont Tremblant's many lakes reflects autumn's vivid colours.

122 The Eastern Townships, or l'Estrie, provide an idyllic setting for fields and farmhouses, winding dirt roads, and country inns.

123 A short trip outside of bustling Montreal brings one to the tranquillity of the countryside, where autumn splashes a palette of exuberant colour across the landscape.

124/125 In summer, Bromont is the site of the Equestrian Olympics.

126/127 Children pass a lazy day fishing in one of the many lakes in the Eastern Townships.